Revised Edition

Ten Basic *Responsibilities* of Nonprofit Boards

Richard T. Ingram

Book One of the BoardSource Governance Series

Formerly the National Center for Nonprofit Boards

Library of Congress Cataloging-in-Publication Data

Ingram, Richard T., 1941

Ten basic responsibilities of nonprofit
 boards / by Richard T. Ingram.
 p. cm. — (Governance series)

Includes bibliographical references and index.
 ISBN 1-58686-054-2

1. Nonprofit organizations — Management.
2. Associations, institutions, etc. — Management.
3. Directors of corporations.
I. Title: 10 basic responsibilities of nonprofit boards.
II. Title.
III. Governance series (BoardSource (Organization))
 HD62.6 .I54 2002
 658.4'22 — dc21
2002012673

© 2003 BoardSource.
First printing, November 2002.

ISBN 1-58686-054-2

This publication may not be reproduced without permission. Permission can be obtained by completing a request for permission form located at www.boardsource.org. Revenue from publications sales ensures the capacity of BoardSource to produce resources and provide services to strengthen the governing boards of nonprofit organizations. Copies of this book and all other BoardSource publications can be ordered by calling 800-883-6262. Discounts are available for bulk purchases.

The views in each BoardSource publication are those of its author and do not represent official positions of BoardSource or its sponsoring organizations.

Building Effective Nonprofit Boards

Formerly the National Center for Nonprofit Boards

BoardSource, formerly the National Center for Nonprofit Boards, is the premier resource for practical information, tools and best practices, training, and leadership development for board members of nonprofit organizations worldwide. Through our highly acclaimed programs and services, BoardSource enables organizations to fulfill their missions by helping build strong and effective nonprofit boards.

BoardSource provides assistance and resources to nonprofit leaders through workshops, training, and our extensive Web site, www.boardsource.org. A team of BoardSource governance consultants works directly with nonprofit leaders to design specialized solutions to meet organizations' needs and assists nongovernmental organizations around the world through partnerships and capacity building. As the world's largest, most comprehensive publisher of materials on nonprofit governance, BoardSource offers a wide selection of books, videotapes, and CDs. BoardSource also hosts the National Leadership Forum, bringing together approximately 800 governance experts, board members, and chief executives of nonprofit organizations from around the world.

Created out of the nonprofit sector's critical need for governance guidance and expertise, BoardSource is a 501(c)(3) nonprofit organization that has provided practical solutions to nonprofit organizations of all sizes in diverse communities. In 2001, BoardSource changed its name from the National Center for Nonprofit Boards to better reflect its mission. Today, BoardSource has more than 15,000 members and has served more than 75,000 nonprofit leaders.

For more information, please visit our Web site at www.boardsource.org, e-mail us at mail@boardsource.org, or call us at 800-883-6262.

HAVE YOU USED THESE BOARDSOURCE RESOURCES?

VIDEOS

Meeting the Challenge: An Orientation to Nonprofit Board Service

Speaking of Money: A Guide to Fund-Raising for Nonprofit Board Members

Building a Successful Team: A Guide to Nonprofit Board Development

BOOKS

The Board Chair Handbook

Managing Conflicts of Interest: Practical Guidelines for Nonprofit Boards

Checks and Balances: The Board Member's Guide to Nonprofit Financial Audits

The Board-Savvy CEO: How To Build a Strong, Positive Relationship with Your Board

Presenting: Board Orientation

Presenting: Nonprofit Financials

The Board Meeting Rescue Kit: 20 Ideas for Jumpstarting Your Board Meetings

The Board Building Cycle: Nine Steps to Finding, Recruiting, and Engaging Nonprofit Board Members

The Policy Sampler: A Resource for Nonprofit Boards

To Go Forward, Retreat! The Board Retreat Handbook

Nonprofit Board Answer Book: Practical Guide for Board Members and Chief Executives

Nonprofit Board Answer Book II: Beyond the Basics

The Legal Obligations of Nonprofit Boards

Self-Assessment for Nonprofit Governing Boards

Assessment of the Chief Executive

Fearless Fundraising

The Nonprofit Board's Guide to Bylaws

Creating and Using Investment Policies

Transforming Board Structure: New Possibilities for Committees and Task Forces

THE GOVERNANCE SERIES

1. *Ten Basic Responsibilities of Nonprofit Boards*
2. *Financial Responsibilities of Nonprofit Boards*
3. *Structures and Practices of Nonprofit Boards*
4. *Fundraising Responsibilities of Nonprofit Boards*
5. *Legal Responsibilities of Nonprofit Boards*
6. *The Nonprofit Board's Role in Setting and Advancing the Mission*
7. *The Nonprofit Board's Role in Planning and Evaluation*
8. *How To Help Your Board Govern More and Manage Less*
9. *Leadership Roles in Nonprofit Governance*

For an up-to-date list of publications and information about current prices, membership, and other services, please call BoardSource at 800-883-6262 or visit our Web site at www.boardsource.org.

Contents

Introduction vii

Chapter 1
Determine the Organization's Mission and Purpose 1

Chapter 2
Select the Chief Executive 2

Chapter 3
Provide Proper Financial Oversight 4

Chapter 4
Ensure Adequate Resources 6

Chapter 5
Ensure Legal and Ethical
Integrity and Maintain Accountability 8

Chapter 6
Ensure Effective Organizational Planning 10

Chapter 7
Recruit and Orient New Board
Members and Assess Board Performance 13

Chapter 8
Enhance the Organization's Public Standing 15

Chapter 9
Determine, Monitor, and Strengthen
the Organization's Programs and Services 17

Chapter 10
Support the Chief Executive and
Assess His or Her Performance 19

Conclusion 21

Appendix I — Statement of Individual Board
Member Responsibilities 22

Appendix II — Summary of the
Ten Basic Responsibilities 25

Appendix III — Basic Responsibilities Worksheet 26

Appendix IV — Suggested Resources 27

About the Author 31

Governance Series Index 32

Introduction

A voluntary spirit and philanthropic instinct permeate most societies in the shape of informal community groups, religious organizations, or charitable nonprofit organizations. Nowhere else does this ethic take on more form and substance than through service on the governing board of a nonprofit, voluntary organization.

The first chapter of this book lists the 10 basic responsibilities of governing nonprofit boards. These functions can be adapted for inclusion in bylaws or other policy documents. They, together with the individual board member's responsibilities in Appendix I, offer criteria against which to review performance and to ensure a measure of accountability. A summary of these 10 responsibilities can be found in Appendix II, and a worksheet for assessing how well your board fulfills these responsibilities is available in Appendix III. Appendix IV is a list of suggested resources for more information on the responsibilities of nonprofit boards and their members.

The functions of governing boards are receiving increasing attention. The volume of information available on nonprofit governance continues to grow. Board members are reading more, programs of board development are more commonplace, and there is growing acceptance of the notion that effective governance determines organizational effectiveness. The purpose of this book is to clarify and distinguish the responsibilities of the board as a collective entity and those of individual board members. The first step to effective board service is to reduce the many ambiguities that inevitably accompany it.

This book reflects five assumptions toward this end:

1. Although every organization is unique, and there is no one-size-fits-all model to governance, there are fundamental responsibilities that hold true for almost every board.

2. How boards and board members actually fulfill their responsibilities will vary depending on the organization's size, structure, and history.

3. No generic model of board size, composition, or structure has proven itself viable in all circumstances. On the other hand, a body of knowledge has evolved that argues for certain structures, policies, and practices that consistently work better than others.

4. All organizations undergo a metamorphosis that calls for periodic evaluation, fine-tuning, and sometimes major overhaul of their governance structures. Organizational performance, like human performance, is cyclical in effectiveness and needs renewal as it evolves over time.

5. Boards and board members perform best when they exercise their responsibilities primarily by asking good, timely questions rather than by managing programs or implementing their own policies. The relationship between the board and staff tends to be strongest when expectations are mutual and responsibilities are clear.

1. DETERMINE THE ORGANIZATION'S MISSION AND PURPOSE

The board is fundamentally responsible for defining the organization's mission and what it strives to accomplish. A commitment to the organization's mission should drive the board's sense of public accountability. This usually takes the form of a written mission statement. In addition to ensuring that the organization has an up-to-date statement of what it is, represents, and does, the board should periodically review the mission statement's adequacy, accuracy, and validity. Although the board is wise to consult with the organization's stakeholders — such as its members, volunteers, staff, clients served, or national or state offices — when revising or updating the organization's mission, it is ultimately the board's responsibility to adopt it. A widely distributed statement of mission and purpose should articulate what the organization does, why it does it, and whom it serves. It should explain what makes the organization distinctive and special and present a compelling reason for individuals, foundations, and corporations to support it financially.

An adequate statement of mission and purpose should serve as a guide to organizational planning, board and staff decision making, volunteer initiatives, and setting priorities among competing demands for scarce resources. The board should assess program activities against the mission to ensure that the organization is not drifting away from its original purposes. The mission sets the stage for developing fundraising strategies and strategic planning as well as the board's many other responsibilities.

For more information on determining the organization's mission and purpose, see The Nonprofit Board's Role in Setting and Advancing the Mission, *book 6 in the Boardsource Governance Series.*

Questions the Board Should Ask

1. What is our mission and purpose?

2. When was the last time the board discussed the adequacy of the mission statement?

3. How do we communicate our mission and purpose with stakeholders?

2 SELECT THE CHIEF EXECUTIVE

The responsibility of choosing the chief executive undoubtedly has the greatest impact on the organization's development and effectiveness. While this function may also be shared with others who have a stake in the outcome, the final decision is, and should be, the board's to make.

The board may choose to hire an executive search consultant to help recruit a strong field of candidates, or it may prefer to execute the search on its own. A carefully considered search process is essential, of course, but in order for a chief executive to perform effectively, the board must recognize its duty to provide a positive working environment. Prior to a search process, the board should

- review the organization's statement of mission and purpose and ensure its adequacy

- conduct an inventory of the organization's major strengths and needs

- establish specific long-term priorities for the next period of executive leadership

- establish clear objectives and clarify expectations for at least the first year of the new chief executive's service

- articulate the particular characteristics, skills, and style it seeks in its new chief executive

- provide an adequate compensation package and other employment terms

- clarify its own functions as distinct from those of the chief executive and staff, including recognizing the chief executive's exclusive responsibility to select and supervise a management team without board interference

- prepare a comprehensive job description that reaffirms that the organization's chief executive is the chief *staff* officer (by whatever title). There should be no ambiguity with the position of the top elected *board* officer on this matter.

For more information on the hiring the chief executive, see Leadership Roles in Nonprofit Governance, *book 9 in the Boardsource Governance Series.*

Questions the Board Should Ask

1. How do board and chief executive responsibilities differ?

2. What are our expectations for our chief executive? What are his expectations of the board?

3. Looking at the strengths and weaknesses of our organization, what kinds of skills and expertise do we need in our next chief executive?

3 PROVIDE PROPER FINANCIAL OVERSIGHT

Boards traditionally exercise this responsibility by helping to develop and approve the annual budget. Indeed, this annual rite is probably one of the board's most significant policy decisions because it sets in motion a host of programmatic, personnel, and other priorities. This responsibility should not be delegated to the board's executive or finance committees.

The board can only monitor the budget's implementation if it is provided clear, intelligible, accurate, and timely financial reports. All board members should receive regular (at least quarterly) balance sheets with a consolidated accounting of all assets and current liabilities. The board treasurer or finance committee should see financial statements even more frequently. All of these reports should show comparative figures for the same period in the preceding fiscal year, and, above all, they should be comprehensible to board members. Board members should not shy away from suggesting improvements in the formats and presentations of financial reports or asking clarifying questions.

The board should insist on an annual audit by an independent auditor. A volunteer board member should never perform the audit function. As the auditors are directly responsible to the board, it is good practice for the board's audit committee to meet with the auditor at least subsequent to the audit process and before the audit is in its final form. The audit committee should be made up of people not on the finance committee. The finance committee should not hire or oversee the audit or the auditors, as it is, in part, this committee's work that is being audited.

Boards of larger organizations sometimes make specific requests before the audit process begins. For instance, the board may give instructions concerning one or two areas or questions for inclusion in the auditor's management letter that is prepared for the board and chief executive separately from the audit report. Finally, all board members should receive the audit report prior to the meeting at which it is discussed and voted upon. The audit committee is responsible for selecting the auditor, reviewing the auditor's performance, and deciding when it is time for a new auditor (approximately every three to five years).

Several other functions are part of the board's responsibility of managing the nonprofit organization's resources effectively, including ensuring that the requisite cash-management controls are in place and monitoring the performance of key staff members such as the chief financial officer.

Board financial responsibilities include purchasing adequate liability insurance, monitoring the distribution of authority for financial decisions between the board and staff, and overseeing investments.

The board monitors the organization's reserve funds and endowments and formulates investment policy and strategy. The board should seek external investment advice when it is needed.

For more information on the board's role in providing proper financial oversight, see Financial Responsibilities of Nonprofit Boards, *book 2 in the Boardsource Governance Series.*

Questions the Board Should Ask

1. How closely do we monitor our financial activity compared with what was budgeted?

2. What internal controls are in place in our organization?

3. What is our strategy to ensure the long-term financial health of the organization?

4 Ensure Adequate Resources

An organization can only be effective if it has enough resources to meet its purposes. Providing adequate resources is first and foremost a board responsibility. Many organizations confuse the chief executive's and the board's responsibilities on this score, particularly when the staff includes a director of development or fundraiser.

It is perfectly appropriate to consider the chief executive as the chief fundraiser, but the board should help to set fundraising goals. The performance of the board, chief executive, and director of development is intimately linked to board members and their ability to influence potentially large donors and otherwise monitor and guide fundraising initiatives. Effective fundraising is one measure of the board's capabilities, commitment, and influence. Every board member should examine his or her connections with potentially helpful givers, and the board should accept responsibility in this area. In addition to soliciting gifts from individuals, corporations, foundations, or governments, board members can help the organization's fundraising efforts by cultivating interest in the organization among potential donors and thanking and maintaining relationships with donors after gifts have been made.

The board should periodically consider and approve a fundraising case statement — a written statement of the need that stems from the organization's mission and goals. The case should clearly explain why the organization needs money and how it will be used.

In organizations that solicit funds from individuals, all board members should make an annual gift aligned with their means. Their personal and collective example is very important. In addition to being able to report 100-percent board participation to potential and current supporters, board members are better fundraisers when they know they are doing their parts.

The board should guard against a natural tendency to behave as if its development or fundraising committee alone bears the responsibility for fundraising. Again, fundraising is a full board function; the appropriate standing committee is simply the board's agent to help oversee the work of board members, the chief executive, and any fundraising staff. Board member complacency should not be tolerated. Indeed, one of the development committee's functions is to remind all board members of their responsibilities.

Although fundraising plays an integral part in ensuring adequate resources for an organization to function, the board's responsibility goes beyond members' function as fundraisers. The board must ensure the organization's current revenues are stable and encourage the cultivation of sources of revenue that are sustainable for the long term. For instance, the board may advocate the creation of revenue-generating activities that have the potential for growth, such as income from publication sales, membership dues, and other appropriate fees. Entrepreneurial leadership is required today as never before.

For more information on the board's fundraising responsibilities, see Fundraising Responsibilities of Nonprofit Boards, *book 4 in the Boardsource Governance Series.*

Questions the Board Should Ask

1. What is our policy on board member participation in fundraising?
2. How can board members best help our organization's fundraising efforts?
3. Who do we know from our professional or personal lives that could be potential funders for this organization?

5 ENSURE LEGAL AND ETHICAL INTEGRITY AND MAINTAIN ACCOUNTABILITY

Nonprofit organizations have come under increased scrutiny in recent years, caused in part by a few organizations that have failed to maintain appropriate oversight and therefore fell victim to fraud, embezzlement, or some other breach of the public trust. The board is ultimately responsible for ensuring adherence to legal standards and ethical norms. By being diligent in its responsibilities, the board can protect the organization from legal action, promote a safe and ethical working environment, and safeguard the organization's integrity in pursuit of its mission.

One of the marks of an effectively managed and governed organization is its ability to avoid having its board adjudicate personnel issues except in the rarest of circumstances. Solid personnel policies and procedures, grievance protocols, and especially clear understanding about the chief executive's responsibility for hiring, developing, and releasing staff help to ensure proper decorum in this area. Although the board must delegate sufficient authority to the chief executive to handle personnel decisions, there are times when the chief executive needs the board's counsel or when his or her judgment is appropriately challenged. The wise chief executive knows when to consult with the board and ask for its judgment involving disputes not otherwise manageable within the chief executive's prerogatives.

Although laws, IRS requirements, and charity watchdog groups establish certain standards governing nonprofit organizations, effective nonprofits go beyond what is minimally required to maintain accountability.

In its efforts to ensure accountability and legal and ethical behavior, the board establishes policies to guide the organization's board members and staff. Conflict-of-interest policies, for instance, outline acceptable and unacceptable relationships among the organization, its board members, and its staff.

In addition to establishing pertinent policies, the board also is responsible for adhering to provisions of the organization's bylaws and articles of incorporation. A board that acts inconsistently with its own governance documents and adopted policies is very vulnerable to criticism — or worse.

Although the board develops policies, many of the individual accountability maintenance activities fall to staff. But among the activities the board is ultimately responsible for and cannot delegate, are these:

- adhering to local, state, and federal laws and regulations that apply to nonprofit organizations
- filing and making available accurate, timely reports required by federal, state, and local government agencies, including IRS Form 990
- keeping detailed records of any lobbying expenditures and activities
- protecting the organization's staff, volunteers, and clients from harm or injury by ensuring compliance with occupational, safety, health, labor, and related regulations
- developing and maintaining adequate personnel policies and procedures (including grievance mechanisms)
- registering with the appropriate state agency before beginning an organized fundraising campaign
- adhering to the provisions of the organization's bylaws and articles of incorporation and amending them when necessary
- providing for an independent annual audit of all revenues, assets, expenditures, and liabilities
- publishing an annual report that details the organization's mission, programs, board members, and financial condition

For more information on the legal and ethical responsibilities, see Legal Responsibilities of Nonprofit Boards, *book 5 in the Boardsource Governance Series.*

Questions the Board Should Ask

1. How does the board ensure the organization keeps up to date on laws and regulations affecting nonprofit organizations?
2. Is every board member familiar with the organization's bylaws, and are we adhering to them?
3. Do we have clear and appropriate organizational policies?
4. Are we keeping organized and accurate records in case they are requested by government agencies?

6 ENSURE EFFECTIVE ORGANIZATIONAL PLANNING

The planning process enables the board and staff to translate the broad mission of the organization into objectives and goals that can be measured and accomplished. The conventional wisdom is that boards should insist that comprehensive organizational planning is done and done effectively. The perplexing questions for board and staff are: Who should carry out strategic planning, and how can busy volunteer board members meaningfully be involved in the process? Opinions differ on how these questions should be answered, but there is wide unanimity on at least three principles.

First, board members must be involved extensively in the strategic planning process if they are to assume proper ownership of the plan and otherwise help to implement many of the plan's goals and objectives, including the acquisition of new resources. Their role is essentially one of asking good questions, expecting good answers, and serving as resources in areas of personal and professional expertise. Second, board members can be engaged in specific areas of the plan by serving on standing committees or temporary task forces.

Third, the board should formally and enthusiastically approve the plan following an extended period of consultation and opportunity for revision. While some long-range forecasts can be made, it is probably best not to cover more than a three-year period. Annual progress reports by the chief executive will keep the staff accountable and the board aware of progress on priorities.

When there is professional staff, the conduct and coordination of planning is best entrusted to it. We should not expect volunteer board members to be full-time authorities on programmatic, financial, and managerial issues, or to commit to more and longer meetings. The organization's chief executive and staff must share at least as much enthusiasm and ownership as does the board, and perhaps even more because they bear the primary responsibility for implementing the plan.

This is not at all to minimize the board's vital involvement in the planning process, however. Because board members are, or should be, free of vested interest and are responsible for considering issues and rendering judgments for the organization as a whole, and because they must ultimately assess the quality of the goals and objectives resulting from the process, they should be involved extensively in it.

Planning occurs at various levels within an organization depending on its size and complexity, the attitudes of the chief executive, staff, and board concerning its relative importance and any other circumstances. It is the process of conducting a substantive planning effort — of bringing many people together under good leadership — that is often as important as the resulting plan itself. Depending on the special circumstances, mission, and purposes of the organization, most long-range or strategic plans will include some variation and combination of these elements:

- statement of mission and purposes
- assumptions about the future (likely internal and external circumstances)
- current programs and services
- new programs and services
- membership development and retention strategies (if appropriate)
- staffing (current and projected)
- board of directors (size, method of selection, committee structure, other bylaw provisions)
- financial projections (income and expenditures)
- fundraising strategies
- public relations strategies

For more information on planning, see The Nonprofit Board's Role in Planning and Evaluation, *book 7 in the Boardsource Governance Series.*

Questions the Board Should Ask

1. Are the plan's underlying assumptions about the organization and its external environment comprehensive and plausible? Are any major factors missing?

2. What are the cost–benefit ratios for each of the organization's current programs and services? Are any peripheral to the organization's primary purposes? Which should be retained? Which should be discontinued or modified?

3. Looking at recent income and expenditure trends, how realistic are projections? What goal should the organization strive to achieve for financial reserves (e.g., at least one-half of its operating budget)?

4. Are new priorities clear and the proposed means of paying for them realistic? Which can or should be self-supporting and which should be operated at a loss?

7 RECRUIT AND ORIENT NEW BOARD MEMBERS AND ASSESS BOARD PERFORMANCE

All boards have a responsibility to articulate and make known their needs in terms of member experience, skills, influence, demographic, and many other considerations that define a balanced board composition. All boards also have responsibility to properly orient new board members and to periodically and comprehensively assess the board's effectiveness. But there is a related responsibility that more boards are recognizing and acting on — the responsibility to assess the performance of individual board members eligible for reelection or reappointment. None of these are easy matters; all are important.

A distinction needs to be made between two more-or-less equal parts of a comprehensive orientation program: (1) orientation *to the board* and *board membership* — core responsibilities, bylaw provisions, committee structure, meeting practices, what is expected of all board members, and the like; and (2) orientation *to the organization* — its mission, programs and services, goals and aspirations, fundraising strategies, staffing structure and personalities, finances, emerging issues and opportunities, and the like. Trying to do it all in two or three hours is unrealistic.

For boards that have the authority to fill their own vacancies, the most important committee to the long-term health of the board (and, therefore, the organization itself) is the governance committee. This is the board committee that — in consultation with the full board and the chief executive — oversees the process of defining membership needs, cultivates prospective nominees, checks prospective nominee credentials and performance on other nonprofit boards, recruits nominees, oversees the orientation program, and designs programs of board self-assessment. Service on the governance committee entails a very full job description, indeed, one that calls for the board's most committed and respected members to constitute the committee's membership.

This is also the committee that is increasingly called upon by the board to draft a statement of board member responsibilities for subsequent consideration and adoption. Boards are finding such statements to be very helpful with new member recruitment and orientation, and also for use as a frame of reference in reviewing the contributions of incumbent board members who are eligible for reappointment or reelection. Attendance, personal giving, and solicitation records are part of the candid conversations that need to take place, conversations that are devoid of dysfunctional politeness, yet fair and sensitive to the individuals involved.

Usually the governance committee also the leads the board in a self-assessment process every three to five years. During a self-assessment, the board and chief executive stand back from their usual preoccupations and reflect on how well the board is meeting its responsibilities. This process should include a look at how the board's composition, process of identifying and recruiting prospective board members, committee structure, meetings, relationships with key constituencies, and overall performance can be strengthened.

A candid and anonymous written survey of board member perceptions in advance of a workshop or retreat, perhaps supplemented with telephone interviews of at least some board members, can pave the way for consensus on priorities. A qualified third-party facilitator can bring experience, objectivity, credibility, and perspective — along with some innocence — to the process. An overnight stay away from the organization's boardroom combined with opportunities to socialize can build camaraderie and trust among board members and between the board and the chief executive.

For more information on board development, see Structures and Practices of Nonprofit Boards *and* How To Help Your Board Govern More and Manage Less, *books 6 and 8 in the Boardsource Governance Series.*

Questions the Board Should Ask

1. How can we improve orientation for new board members?

2. What skills, expertise, and personal traits should we look for in new board members?

3. When was the last time our board conducted a self-assessment? How were the results used to improve board performance? When do we plan to conduct another self-assessment?

8 ENHANCE THE ORGANIZATION'S PUBLIC STANDING

Board members serve not only as a link between the organization's staff or volunteers and its members, constituents, or clients, but also as the organization's ambassadors, advocates, and community representatives. But government leaders, the media, and current and potential funding sources call for an ambitious and effective public relations program to ensure a healthy and accurate public image for the organization. Clearly articulated achievements, contributions to the public good, and explanations for how gifts and grants and other revenue sources are allocated are all part of the process. Written annual reports, timely and informative press releases, consistent communication initiatives with community and government leaders, and timely speeches by appropriate board members to civic and community groups are important elements of a comprehensive public awareness strategy. Over the course of their tenure, board members may meet with elected officials, testify before legislatures, court foundation program officers, speak to community groups, represent the organization at national forums, and — when appropriate — be interviewed by news media.

One of the most important decisions to be made by the chief executive and the board chair is who should be the organization's spokesperson. This decision normally depends on the situation, but there are advantages on some issues to ask an especially articulate board chair to serve this important function. Volunteer leaders who convey their commitment and dedication through advocacy and a willingness, on behalf of their boards, to get out in front of their chief executives and staffs on the thorny issues, command more public attention and respect because board members do not receive remuneration.

Boards, however, should guard against the occasionally overzealous board member who may take inappropriate and unilateral initiatives without clearance. The board's elected leaders should ensure that the board appropriately disciplines itself. No board member should represent himself or herself as speaking for the board or organization unless specifically authorized to do so.

For more on the communicating with the public about your organization, see, The Nonprofit Board's Role in Setting and Advancing the Mission *and* How To Help Your Board Govern More and Manage Less, *books 6 and 8 in the BoardSource Governance Series.*

Questions the Board Should Ask

1. Who is our organization's spokesperson?

2. What should the spokesperson consider before responding to media inquiries?

3. What should board members other than the board chair do when contacted by the media?

4. What is our organization's communications strategy?

5. What are the key messages we wish to communicate to the public?

9 DETERMINE, MONITOR, AND STRENGTHEN THE ORGANIZATION'S PROGRAMS AND SERVICES

The board's fundamental responsibility begins with the question of whether current and proposed programs and services are consistent with the organization's stated mission and purpose. Given limited resources and unlimited demands on them, the board must decide among competing priorities. Financial and programmatic decisions should not be made independently.

What the organization does for its members, constituents, or clients determines its significance as a social institution. Yet, there is nearly universal complaint by board members that their meeting agendas are dominated by finance and fundraising issues. Every board must find a sensible division of labor among its members to ensure that programs and services are demonstrably consistent with the organization's mission and purposes and are of high quality. This minimally argues for a standing committee to oversee programs.

The board should have a good sense of its monitoring and oversight role by seeking a balance between the board's responsibility to ensure quality, cost-effective programs and services and the staff's responsibility to creatively initiate and conduct them. In meeting this particular responsibility, board and staff roles often become confused, particularly when board members also volunteer extensively to conduct and manage programs. Candor, openness, and explicit job descriptions go a long way toward negotiating an accommodation satisfactory to everyone.

Here again, the board best performs its role by asking the right questions and expecting good answers.

For more information on monitoring programs, see The Nonprofit Board's Role in Planning and Evaluation, *book 7 in the Boardsource Governance Series* .

Questions the Board Should Ask

1. How can the board and staff monitor constituent satisfaction with current and future programs and services?

2. What do we know about who participates in or takes advantage of each of our major programs and services? Are participation trends in the right direction in terms of both numbers and categories of people served?

3. What proportion of the annual budget is devoted to programs and services as distinct from personnel costs and other expenditures?

10. Support the Chief Executive and Assess His or Her Performance

The chief executive needs consistent moral and substantive support from the board. Some boards have found it useful to assign the responsibility for assessing the chief executive's performance to the executive committee. This helps, but the board as a whole should ensure that the chief executive

- receives frequent and constructive feedback
- is assisted when board members overstep prerogatives or misunderstand their roles
- feels that his or her performance is being assessed in relation to the board's performance
- is introduced to other community leaders and organizations
- is invited to important social functions
- is complimented for exceptional initiatives
- is encouraged to take professional and personal leaves for renewal
- feels that the board is aware of and sensitive to personal situations and needs

With regard to informal and formal performance reviews, the board and chief executive should agree on purposes and processes. This delicate business is helped immeasurably if annual goals and objectives are mutually discussed and agreed on; they become the primary criteria for review through informal and candid discussion.

The formal, periodic, and comprehensive review process can be especially challenging for everyone concerned. The board performs this function best, as part of its responsibility to be supportive, when the board and chief executive have agreed on these three points:

1. The primary purpose of the evaluation is to help the chief executive perform more effectively. (Ideally, to keep the process healthy and constructive, compensation increases and contract renewal decisions should *not* be the *primary* purpose for conducting the process.)

2. The chief executive should be consulted on the process of review well before it is initiated.

3. The board and chief executive need to understand their effectiveness is interdependent — neither can be assessed completely independently.

Given the importance and delicacy of comprehensive executive performance assessment, and assuming performance reviews will be conducted at regular intervals by standing board policy, many boards and executives have found it useful to secure mutually agreed-upon and qualified third-party services from outside the organization. Such an initiative, perhaps every three to five years, brings professionalism, objectivity, and perspective that almost always justify the required financial investment. An outside person acceptable to the chief executive and the board can assess both chief executive performance and any organizational or governance constraints and make recommendations helpful to everyone.

For more information on the hiring the chief executive, see Leadership Roles in Nonprofit Governance, *book 9 in the Boardsource Governance Series.*

Questions the Board Should Ask

1. What is our policy for evaluating the chief executive's performance? Is the chief executive aware of this policy?

2. What is our process for evaluating the chief executive's performance? Is the chief executive aware of this process?

3. Who is responsible for communicating with the chief executive about and during this process?

Conclusion

There are other board responsibilities, of course. Students of governance all have their favorite lists. It is important and useful, however, to make a distinction between *board* and *board member* responsibilities. Written job descriptions for the board and for its members should help boards to strengthen their sense of purpose, relations with chief executive and staff, organization and structure, and overall performance. This book concludes with a sample of individual board member's responsibilities that can be adapted to various organizational settings.

Boards and their members continue to be underdeveloped resources — in part because it is natural to respond only to expectations held for them, and in part because of the ambiguities inherent in board responsibilities and board-staff relations. Furthermore, some chief executives and some boards are ambivalent or even negative about in-service education and board development programs. After all, some risk taking is involved; inviting a third party to help with the process, for example, can be a difficult decision indeed.

Boards are learning to balance their nearly limitless organizational powers with self-restraint, to delegate authority where possible and sensible without abdicating their considerable responsibilities, and to channel board member enthusiasm and commitment into appropriate behaviors. As nonprofit organizations continue to evolve and strengthen their governance practices, the entire sector will surely strengthen its already significant contributions to the communities it serves.

Appendix I

STATEMENT OF INDIVIDUAL BOARD MEMBER RESPONSIBILITIES

Just as boards of directors have basic collective responsibilities, **individual board members are also entrusted with responsibilities** as a part of board membership. The obligations of board service are considerable — they extend well beyond the basic expectations of attending meetings, participating in fundraising initiatives, and making monetary contributions.

A clear statement of individual board member responsibilities adapted to the organization's needs and circumstances can serve at least two purposes: (1) It can help with the process of recruiting new board members by clarifying expectations before candidates accept nomination, and (2) it can provide criteria by which the committee responsible for identifying and recruiting prospective nominees can review the performance of incumbents who are eligible for reelection or reappointment.

Prospective and incumbent board members should commit themselves to the following responsibilities.

GENERAL EXPECTATIONS

- Know the organization's mission, purpose, goals, policies, programs, services, strengths, and needs.

- Perform duties of board membership responsibly and conform to the level of competence expected from board members as outlined in the duties of care, loyalty, and obedience as they apply to nonprofit board members.

- Suggest possible nominees to the board who are clearly women and men of achievement and distinction and who can make significant contributions to the work of the board and the organization's progress.

- Serve in leadership positions and undertake special assignments willingly and enthusiastically.

- Avoid prejudiced judgments on the basis of information received from individuals and urge those with grievances to follow established policies and procedures through their supervisors. (All matters of potential significance should be called to the attention of the executive and the board's elected leader as appropriate.)

- Follow trends in the organization's field of interest.
- Bring good will and a sense of humor to the board's deliberations.

Meetings

- Prepare for and participate in board and committee meetings, including appropriate organizational activities.
- Ask timely and substantive questions at board and committee meetings consistent with your conscience and convictions, while supporting the majority decision on issues decided by the board.
- Maintain confidentiality of the board's executive sessions, and speak for the board or organization only when authorized to do so.
- Suggest agenda items periodically for board and committee meetings to ensure that significant, policy-related matters are addressed.

Relationship with Staff

- Counsel the chief executive as appropriate and support him or her through often difficult relationships with groups or individuals.
- Avoid asking for special favors of the staff, including special requests for extensive information, without at least prior consultation with the chief executive, board, or appropriate committee chairperson.

Avoiding Conflicts

- Serve the organization as a whole rather than any special interest group or constituency. Regardless of whether or not you were invited to fill a vacancy reserved for a certain constituency or organization, your first obligation is to avoid any preconception that you "represent" anything but the organization's best interests.
- Avoid even the appearance of a conflict of interest that might embarrass the board or the organization, and disclose any possible conflicts to the board in a timely fashion.
- Maintain independence and objectivity and do what a sense of fairness, ethics, and personal integrity dictate, even though not necessarily obliged to do so by law, regulation, or custom.
- Never accept (or offer) favors or gifts from (or to) anyone who does business with the organization.

FIDUCIARY RESPONSIBILITIES

- Exercise prudence with the board in the control and transfer of funds.
- Faithfully read and understand the organization's financial statements and otherwise help the board fulfill its fiduciary responsibility.

FUNDRAISING

- Give an annual gift according to personal means.
- Assist the development committees and staff by implementing fundraising strategies through personal influence with others (corporations, individuals, foundations).

Appendix II

THE BOARDSOURCE TEN BASIC RESPONSIBILITIES

1. **Determine the organization's mission and purpose.** It is the board's responsibility to create and review a statement of mission and purpose that articulates the organization's goals, means, and primary constituents served.

2. **Select the chief executive.** Boards must reach consensus on the chief executive's responsibilities and undertake a careful search to find the most qualified individual for the position.

3. **Provide proper financial oversight.** The board must assist in developing the annual budget and ensuring that proper financial controls are in place.

4. **Ensure adequate resources.** One of the board's foremost responsibilities is to provide adequate resources for the organization to fulfill its mission.

5. **Ensure legal and ethical integrity and maintain accountability.** The board is ultimately responsible for ensuring adherence to legal standards and ethical norms.

6. **Ensure effective organizational planning.** Boards must actively participate in an overall planning process and assist in implementing and monitoring the plan's goals.

7. **Recruit and orient new board members and assess board performance.** All boards have a responsibility to articulate prerequisites for candidates, orient new members, and periodically and comprehensively evaluate its own performance.

8. **Enhance the organization's public standing.** The board should clearly articulate the organization's mission, accomplishments, and goals to the public and garner support from the community.

9. **Determine, monitor, and strengthen the organization's programs and services.** The board's responsibility is to determine which programs are consistent with the organization's mission and to monitor their effectiveness.

10. **Support the chief executive and assess his or her performance.** The board should ensure that the chief executive has the moral and professional support he or she needs to further the goals of the organization.

Appendix III

Basic Responsibilities Worksheet

Use this worksheet to assess how well your board fulfills its basic responsibilities.

Responsibility	My board supports this responsibility by	My board could improve in this area by
1. Determine the organization's mission and purpose		
2. Select the chief executive		
3. Provide proper financial oversight		
4. Ensure adequate funding		
5. Ensure legal and ethical integrity and maintain accountability		
6. Ensure effective organizational planning		
7. Recruit and orient new board members and assess board performance		
8. Enhance the organization's public standing		
9. Determine, monitor, and strengthen the organization's programs and services		
10. Support the chief executive and assess his or her performance		

Appendix IV

SUGGESTED RESOURCES

Albert, Sheila. *Hiring the Chief Executive: A Practical Guide to the Search and Selection Process.* Washington, DC: BoardSource, 2000. Hiring a new chief executive is one of the most important tasks a board must undertake. This book presents a model for the process that can easily be adapted by almost any nonprofit organization. The book stresses the importance of legal advice, identifies the most important characteristics of the next chief executive, and provides valuable questions for the candidate-interviewing process. It also includes a sample job description and a system for rating candidates. The revised version comes with a diskette with sample forms and worksheets.

Axelrod, Nancy. *Chief Executive Succession Planning: The Board's Role in Securing Your Organization's Future.* Washington, DC: BoardSource, 2002. Chief executive succession planning is not only about determining your organization's next leader. It is a continuous process that assesses your organization's needs and identifies leadership that supports those needs. A successful succession plan is linked to your organization's strategic plan, mission, and vision. Author Nancy Axelrod helps board members prepare for the future by examining the ongoing and intermittent steps of executive succession planning.

BoardSource. *Self-Assessment for Nonprofit Governing Boards.* Washington, DC: BoardSource, 1999. This assessment book is designed to help nonprofit boards determine how well they're carrying out their responsibilities and identify areas that need improvement. This evaluation toolkit includes a user's guide and 15 board member questionnaires so that you can easily distribute the resource to your board.

Bobowick, Marla, Sandra Hughes, and Berit Lakey. *Transforming Board Structure: Strategies for Committees and Task Forces.* Washington, DC: BoardSource, 2001. This book provides a fresh look at committees and how your board can use work groups to streamline the work of the full board. Discover the importance of reducing the number of standing committees and relying more on ad hoc groups and task forces.

Chait, Richard P. *How To Help Your Board Govern More and Manage Less.* Washington, DC: BoardSource, 2003. Is your board managing instead of governing? Understanding this distinction will increase your board's ability to work effectively. Discover how your board can successfully work with staff, and how this dynamic changes as the size of your organization's staff changes. Also included are specific procedures to strengthen your board's capacity to govern.

Dambach, Charles F. *Structures and Practices of Nonprofit Boards*. Washington, DC: BoardSource, 2003. Looking for ways to improve efficiency? Help your board members keep long-term goals and board development at the forefront of their work. Included are practical guidelines on structural issues, such as running meetings, committee structure, size of the board, and term limits. Improve the way that your board works by increasing flexibility and improving interpersonal relationships.

Gale, Robert L. *Leadership Roles in Nonprofit Governance*. Washington, DC: BoardSource, 2003. Strong nonprofit board leadership is important to the success of your organization. This book clarifies the difference in the roles of the chief executive and board chair and provides suggestions for how this partnership can be strengthened. Discover how this leadership can effectively work with the governance committee to facilitate board development. Don't miss the sample job descriptions and a discussion on "What Keeps the President Awake at Night."

Grace, Kay Sprinkel. *The Nonprofit Board's Role in Setting and Advancing the Mission*. Washington, DC: BoardSource, 2003. Is your board actively supporting and advancing your organization's mission? Learn how board members can actively contribute to the creation of mission as well as communicate the mission and purpose to the community. Discover how your board can actively partner with organizational staff to implement mission and supporting policies.

Greenfield, James. *Fundraising Responsibilities of Nonprofit Boards*. Washington, DC: BoardSource, 2003. Discover why fundraising is important and why board members should be involved. Included are practical suggestions for board members in direction, planning, and oversight of fundraising. Help your board succeed in the three phases of fundraising — cultivation, solicitation, and stewardship.

Hopkins, Bruce R. *Legal Responsibilities of Nonprofit Boards*. Washington, DC: BoardSource, 2003. All board members should understand their legal responsibilities, including when and how they can be held personally liable and what type of oversight they should provide. Discover the essential information that board members should know to protect themselves and their organization. Written in non-technical language, this book provides legal concepts and definitions, as well as a detailed discussion on ethics.

Hughes, Sandra R., Berit M. Lakey and Marla J. Bobowick. *The Board Building Cycle: Nine Steps to Finding, Recruiting and Engaging Board Nonprofit Board Members.* Washington, DC: BoardSource, 2000. This book provides helpful tips on what motivates people to join boards, how and where to find board members, ideas for conducting an orientation session, and specific tasks for the board's governance committee. Also included are suggestions for involving former board members as advisors of committee members and removing difficult or ineffective board members. Included with The Board Building Cycle is a diskette containing worksheets and forms.

Lakey, Berit. *Nonprofit Governance: Steering Your Organization with Authority and Accountability.* Washington, DC: BoardSource, 2000. This book outlines the essentials of nonprofit governance and describes ways that boards and board members can add value to the organizations they serve. BoardSource governance consultant Berit M. Lakey defines the difference between policy making and management and outlines the basic responsibilities of a nonprofit board to set organizational direction, ensure the necessary resources, and provide oversight.

Lang, Andrew S. *Financial Responsibilities of Nonprofit Boards.* Washington, DC: BoardSource, 2003. Provide your board members with an understanding of their financial responsibilities including an overview of financial oversight and ways to ensure against risk. Written in non-technical language, this book will help your board understand financial planning, the IRS Form 990, and the audit process. Also included are financial board and staff job descriptions and charts on all the financial documents and reports, including due dates and filing procedures.

Pierson, Jane, and Joshua Mintz. *Assessment of the Chief Executive: A Tool for Boards and Chief Executives of Nonprofit Organizations.* Washington, DC: BoardSource, 1995. This practical guide to chief executive assessment leads the board and chief executive through a thoughtful discussion about the chief executive's performance and future aspirations. Included are multiple worksheets and questionnaires to guide the process.

Speaking of Money: A Guide to Fund Raising for Nonprofit Board Members. Washington, DC: BoardSource, 1996, 28 minutes. Broadcaster Hugh Downs leads a thoughtful examination of the board's role in the development process. In the video, eight board members representing a diverse group of nonprofits discuss how they raise money for the organizations they serve.

Yankey, John A. and Amy McClellan. *The Nonprofit Board's Role in Planning and Evaluation.* Washington, DC: BoardSource, 2003. Strategic planning and outcome measurement are important issues for every nonprofit board. Learn how your board should be involved in strategic planning and how that plan should link to outcomes measurement. Discover different options for measuring organizational effectiveness and how to analyze both the organization and specific programs. Don't miss the suggestions for dealing with the results of your evaluation.

About the Author

Richard T. Ingram is president of the Association of Governing Boards of Universities and Colleges, a national nonprofit educational association in the service of higher education trustees and chief executives. He serves or has served on the boards of two independent colleges, a secondary school, a higher education association, a multiple-employer trust, and a liability insurance risk retention group. Dr. Ingram has conducted scores of programs for the boards and chief executives of nonprofit organizations, including Independent Sector, American Lung Association, Special Olympics, United Cerebral Palsy Association of California, Appalachian Mountain Club, National Symphony Orchestra, and the American Hospital Association. He is a contributing author and editor of Governing Independent Colleges and Universities (Jossey-Bass, 1994), Effective Trusteeship (AGB, 1995), Presidential and Board Assessment (AGB, 2000), and other publications.

Index

This index references Books One through Nine of the BoardSource Governance Series. Each topic entry is followed by the book number and the page on which that reference appears.

For example, "Accountability, Book 1:8" shows that information on the subject of accountability is found in Book One, on page eight.

A

A-133 audit, Book 2:7

Accountability, Book 1:8; Book 3:1, 4–5; Book 5:2, 12, 23

    nondelegatable board responsibilities, Book 1:8–9

Accountant, Book 9:15

Accounting manual, Book 2:10, 11

Accounting policies and procedures, Book 2:11–12

Accounting restatement, Book 5:23

Accrual accounting, defined, Book 2:38

Action plan, characterized, Book 7:7

Activities, defined, Book 7:39

Ad hoc committee, Book 3:19

Adverse opinion, Book 2:21

Advisory council, Book 3:19; Book 5:10

    rights and duties, Book 5:10

Agenda

    board chair, Book 9:2

    board meeting, Book 3:24–25; Book 9:5

        consent agenda, Book 3:25

        preparation, Book 3:24

        priority items, Book 3:24–25

        reports, Book 3:25

        topics, Book 3:24

    chief executive, Book 9:2

All-volunteer organization, micromanagement, Book 8:5

Amortization, defined, Book 2:38

Annual giving, Book 4:3–4

    benefit, Book 4:4

    by board member, Book 1:6

    direct mail, Book 4:3

    donor club, Book 4:3

    goals, Book 4:3

    groups, guilds, and associations, Book 4:4

    membership program, Book 4:3

    special event, Book 4:4

    telephone contact, Book 4:4

    volunteer-led solicitation, Book 4:4

    Web-based giving, Book 4:4

Annual information return, Book 5:25

Annual operating expenses, Book 4:vii

Annual report, Book 1:9, 15; Book 6:32

Annuity, Book 4:5

Annuity gift, defined, Book 2:38

Appearance of propriety, Book 2:5

Articles of incorporation, Book 1:8, 9; Book 5:7, 18

Assets, Book 2:2

    defined, Book 2:38

Audit, Book 1:4, 9; Book 3:5; Book 9:1–2. *See also* External audit

    A-133 audit, Book 2:7

    adverse opinion, Book 2:21

    audit partner rotation, Book 5:23

    defined, Book 2:20, 38

    disclaimed opinion, Book 2:21

    finance committee, Book 1:4

    Letter of Reportable Conditions, Book 2:21

    Management Letter, Book 2:21

    members' audit, Book 2:12–13

    purpose, Book 3:21

    qualified opinion, Book 2:20–21

    specific requests, Book 1:4

    unplanned auditor turnover, Book 2:23

    unqualified (clean) opinion, Book 2:20, 31

    fourth paragraph in, Book 2:20

year-end
    footnotes, Book 2:19–20
    statement of activities, Book 2:19
    statement of cash flows, Book 2:19
    statement of changes in net assets, Book 2:19
    statement of financial position, Book 2:19

Audit committee
    finance committee, distinguished, Book 3:21
    functions, Book 3:21
    functions of, Book 2:14
    need for, Book 3:21
    responsibilities, Book 1:4

Auditor
    independent, Book 1:4
    insurance, Book 2:6
    internal controls, Book 2:10–11
    rotation, Book 5:23
    selection of, Book 2:12

B

Bank
    bank account types, Book 2:26
    selection of, Book 2:24
    services of, Book 2:24

Benchmark, defined, Book 7:22, 39

Benefit, Book 4:4

Benefits
    board member, Book 2:6
    chief executive, Book 2:5–6
    increasing, Book 2:22
    staff, Book 2:5–6

Bequest, Book 4:5

Board book, Book 5:19–20

Board chair, Book 8:6
    agenda, Book 9:2
    board development, Book 9:2
    board effectiveness as priority of, Book 9:8–9
    board evaluation, Book 9:2
    board meeting, Book 9:2
        leading, Book 9:5
    board orientation, Book 9:2
    board recruitment, Book 9:2
    budget, Book 9:1, 2
    chief executive and, Book 9
        board chair availability, Book 9:6
    building good working relationship between, Book 9:6
    evaluation of, Book 9:6
    informal meetings of, Book 9:6, 11
    committees, Book 9:2
    communications, Book 9:3
    effectiveness, Book 9:5–10
    finances, Book 9:1–2
    financial commitment of, Book 9:8
    fundraising, Book 9:3, 7–8
    information, Book 9:7
    lack of replacement for, Book 9:vii
    meeting, Book 3:14
    micromanagement by, Book 8:5; Book 9:viii
    mission, Book 6:40–41
    policy and planning, Book 9:1
    prospective donor, Book 9:8
    public relations, Book 9:3
    recruiting new board members, Book 9:8, 9
    responsibilities, Book 3:14; Book 8:5
    sample job description, Book 9:18–19
    spokesperson, Book 3:14
    staff oversight, compensation, and evaluation, Book 9:3
    succession, Book 6:40
    understanding of organization, Book 9:7

Board development, Book 1:vii, 21; Book 3:15–17
    Board Development Matrix, Book 3:15, 35
    bylaws, Book 3:15

Board information system, Book 8:17

Board meeting, Book 1:23; Book 3:22–29; Book 8:6
    agenda, Book 3:24–25; Book 9:5
        chief executive, Book 8:7
        consent agenda, Book 3:25; Book 8:10
    preparation, Book 3:24
        prioritized, Book 8:10
        priority items, Book 3:24–25
        reports, Book 3:25
        topics, Book 3:24
    attendance, Book 5:20; Book 9:vii
    board chair, Book 3:14; Book 9:2
    leading, Book 9:5
    board member disaffection, Book 6:39
    board size, Book 3:18
    chief executive, Book 9:2
        agenda, Book 9:13–14
        meeting materials from, Book 8:7
        participation, Book 8:7
        planning of, Book 9:13–14
    conference call, Book 5:9–10
    dashboard report, Book 3:26, 38
    evaluation, Book 3:28–29, 40
    fast-paced, Book 3:7
    fiduciary responsibility, Book 5:20
    frequency, Book 3:22–23; Book 9:14
    meeting cycle, Book 3:23
    meeting materials, Book 3:24; Book 8:6; Book 9:2
        from chief executive, Book 9:14
    minutes, Book 3:26, 28; Book 5:20
        wording of motions, Book 3:28
    mission, Book 3:22
    mission moment at, Book 6:20
    motivation, Book 6:20–21
    new technology for, Book 3:27
    as opportunity for board development, Book 9:5
    organization, Book 3:7
    policy compendium, Book 3:27
    preparation, Book 3:7, 23–24
    proposal, Book 3:26
    Issue Definition and Policy Recommendation system, Book 3:26–27
    purpose, Book 3:22
    quality, Book 6:39–40
    quorum, Book 5:9
    rewards, Book 3:29, 33
    rules of order, Book 3:27–28
    staff participation, Book 8:7; Book 9:14
    success factors of, Book 9:5
    testimonial, Book 6:20
    unanimous written consent, Book 5:9–10
Board member
    action program, Book 5:17–21
    administrative duties of, Book 8:1
    annual gift, Book 1:6
    attributes, Book 3:15
    authority, Book 5:2
    capital campaign, Book 4:7
    personal donation, Book 4:7
    chief executive relationship, Book 9:12
    commitment, Book 8:18
    as community representative, Book 1:15
    competition for, Book 3:2
    demographic factors, Book 3:15
    dissent, Book 5:20
    donor cultivation, Book 4:12
    donor solicitation
        fear of rejection, Book 4:13
        new board member, Book 4:12–13
        preparation, Book 4:13
        rehearsal, Book 4:13
    duty of care, Book 5:3
    duty of loyalty, Book 5:3–4
    duty of obedience, Book 5:4
    election, Book 5:9–10
        from general membership, Book 5:9
    evaluation, Book 1:13
    as fiduciary, Book 5:1–2

filing requirements, Book 5:19
financial commitment, Book 9:8
financial transaction approval, Book 5:19
as fundraiser, Book 1:6–7
fundraising participation worksheet, Book 4:33
fundraising responsibilities, Book 4:34
as guardian of organization's mandate, Book 5:17, 18
ideal, Book 3:12
identifying potential, Book 4:19–21
informal interaction, Book 3:29
information for, Book 9:2
job description, Book 1:21; Book 4:34
lawyer, Book 5:23
liability of, Book 5:1
meeting attendance, Book 5:20
micromanagement by, Book 9:viii
mission, Book 5:17–18
natural tendency to drift into management of, Book 8:1–2
opportunities, Book 6:40–41
organization's legal form and status, Book 5:18–19
orientation
    to board, Book 1:13
        to organization, Book 1:13
        orientation program, Book 8:8–9
as overseer, Book 5:21
performance evaluation, Book 3:16
personal agenda, Book 3:16, 31
personal donation, Book 4:vii, 7, 10–11
reappointment or reelection, Book 1:13
responsibilities, Book 1:8, 13, 22 24; Book 5:1–2
        avoiding conflicts, Book 1:23
        fiduciary responsibilities, Book 1:24
        fundraising, Book 1:24
        general expectations, Book 1:22
        meetings, Book 1:23
        purposes, Book 1:22
    relationship with staff, Book 1:23
    shared understanding of, Book 9:viii
retention, Book 6:39–40
retirement, Book 3:16
role, Book 3:viii; Book 9:viii
satisfaction, Book 8:18
self-perpetuating board, Book 5:9
small vs. large organization, Book 9:1
staff relationship, Book 1:23
micromanagement, Book 9:vii
usefulness of, Book 8:18
written survey of perceptions, Book 1:14
Board of directors, Book 5:26
    accountability, Book 5:2
    adding value to organization, Book 3:12
    advantages of larger, Book 3:18
    advantages of smaller, Book 3:18
    analytical approach, Book 8:15–16
    assumptions, Book 1:viii
    audit by, Book 2:12–13
    benefits, Book 2:6
    characteristics of effective boards, Book 8:14–17
    chief executive
        board support, Book 1:19
        organizational overview, Book 8:7
        relationship, Book 1:2; Book 9:11, 12
    communication, Book 3:20
    composing effective board, Book 3:12–17
    conflict, Book 3:30, 31
    conflict of interest, Book 2:7
    development of, Book 8:14–15
        board chair, Book 9:2
        chief executive, Book 9:2, 13
    disadvantages of larger, Book 3:18
    disruptive members, Book 3:16
    diversity of, Book 3:5; Book 9:8
    education, Book 8:14–15

effective structures, Book 3:18–21
efficient, Book 3:6–7
election process, Book 5:9
emeritus positions, Book 3:19
evaluation, Book 1:13; Book 7:20; Book 9:9
    board chair, Book 9:2
    chief executive, Book 9:2–3
ex officio positions, Book 5:9
feedback on board's performance, Book 8:10–12
finances
    documents board should receive, Book 2:18–22
    financial literacy quiz for, Book 2:34–37
    financial management responsibilities of, Book 2:14
    financial oversight, Book 1:4–5
    financial reports for, Book 1:4
    legal responsibility for, Book 2:14
    private inurement, Book 2:6, 7
    understanding financial condition, Book 2:18–23
functions, Book 7:viii
fundraising
    oversight, Book 4:1–2
    recruitment for, Book 4:19–21
    responsibilities, Book 4:34
goals for, Book 8:15
governance resources, Book 8:19–22
governance responsibilities, Book 8:vii, 8
group norms and standards, Book 8:15
guilt by omission, Book 5:vii
homogeneous, Book 3:12
inappropriately involved in management, Book 8:1
ineffectual, Book 3:30
informed and engaged, Book 8:18
job description, Book 1:21
key indicators of organizational performance, Book 8:7
key responsibilities, Book 7:viii
leadership, Book 8:4, 8, 15
liability, Book 5:2
managing without staff, Book 8:3
micromanagement by, Book 2:23; Book 8:4
mission, Book 6:2–3; Book 8:8
board member agreement, Book 6:19–20
nominating process, Book 3:12, 16
nonprofit organization evaluation, Book 3:6
officers, Book 5:8
organizational effectiveness, Book 7:34
organizational planning, Book 1:10
orientation, Book 3:13–14, 15
    orientation meeting, Book 3:14
    written materials, Book 3:13–14
oversight responsibilities, Book 3:5; Book 4:1–2; Book 5:12
planning, Book 7:viii
program evaluation, Book 7:28
programs and services monitoring, Book 1:17
recruitment
    board chair, Book 9:2
    chief executive, Book 9:2
relationship with constituencies, Book 8:16
responsibilities, Book 1:25; Book 3:vii; Book 5:2
    worksheet, Book 1:26
role, Book 6:18–23
    clarification, Book 8:4
    shared understanding of, Book 9:viii
scope of authority, Book 5:8
self-assessment, Book 3:15, 31–32
    benefits, Book 3:32
    commitment, Book 3:31
    mini self-assessment survey, Book 3:32, 39–41
    outside facilitation, Book 3:32

self-perpetuating board, Book 5:9
size, Book 3:18–19; Book 5:8
specific written and agreed-to objectives for, Book 9:9
sphere of influence, Book 8:vii
staff relationship, Book 1:viii; Book 8:3
role differentiation, Book 8:4–5
as strategic asset, Book 8:18
streamlined, Book 3:6
structures, Book 5:10
three Ds, Book 5:2–4
turnover rates, Book 9:13
unaware of problems, Book 9:vii
venture opportunity evaluation, Book 3:4
why some manage more than govern, Book 8:1–2
work plan, Book 8:8, 17
Board of trustees. See Board of directors
Board recruitment, Book 1:13; Book 3:9, 13, 15; Book 9:8
board chair, Book 9:2
chief executive, Book 9:2
mission, Book 6:36–37, 42
recruitment matrix, Book 6:36
values, Book 6:36–37, 42
Board retreat, Book 5:20
Bonding, Book 2:6, 25; Book 5:15
treasurer, Book 2:15
Bonus, Book 5:23
Bookkeeper, role of, Book 2:16
Boredom, Book 8:18
Budget, Book 1:4
annual, Book 1:4
balancing, Book 2:4–5
board chair, Book 9:1–2
chief executive, Book 9:2
development of, Book 2:1
finance committee, Book 3:20–21
Budget committee, function of, Book 2:14–15
Business interruption insurance, Book 2:6, 25

Business plan
characterized, Book 7:7
defined, Book 7:39
Bylaws, Book 1:8, 9; Book 5:4, 18
board development, Book 3:15
corporation, Book 5:7
indemnification, Book 5:14
rules of order, Book 3:28
strategic planning, Book 7:12
unincorporated association, Book 5:7

C

Capital campaign
board member, Book 4:7
personal donation, Book 4:7
major giving, Book 4:5
Cash, Book 2:11
availability of, Book 2:1–2
investment, Book 2:26
Cash-basis accounting, defined, Book 2:38
Cash-flow projection, Book 2:2
Certified public accountant, Book 5:19
Change, Book 4:8
strategic planning, Book 7:1–2
Charitable giving regulation, Book 5:26
Charitable solicitation act, Book 5:27
Charitable trust, Book 4:5; Book 5:1
Chief executive, Book 5:21, 26
agenda, Book 9:2
benefits, Book 2:5–6
board chair and, Book 9:6
board chair availability, Book 9:6
building relationship between, Book 9:6, 11
informal meetings of, Book 9:6, 11
board chair leadership style and, Book 9:11
board development, Book 9:2, 13
in board effectiveness, Book 9:13
board evaluation, Book 9:2–3
board meeting, Book 9:2
agenda, Book 9:13–14
participation, Book 8:7

planning of, Book 9:13–14
    providing meeting materials, Book 8:7
board of directors
    board support, Book 1:19
    organizational overview, Book 8:7
    relationship, Book 1:2; Book 8:16; Book 9:11–12
board orientation, Book 9:2, 13
board recruitment, Book 9:2
budget, Book 9:2
chair as sounding board for new ideas, Book 9:11
as chief fundraiser, Book 1:6
committees, Book 9:2
communications, Book 9:3, 11
    to board of directors, Book 9:14
    to staff, Book 9:14
compensation, Book 2:5–6
complexities and constraints of, Book 8:18
comprehensive strategic plan, Book 8:6
creating institutional strategy for review by board, Book 8:6
creating strong board-staff partnerships, Book 9:12
evaluation, Book 1:19–20; Book 8:9; Book 9:6
    annual goals and objectives, Book 1:20
    processes, Book 1:20
    by third party, Book 1:20
expectations for, Book 1:2; Book 8:9
finances, Book 9:2, 6, 15
    expert help with, Book 9:15
    financial literacy quiz, Book 2:34–37
    responsibilities in, Book 2:15–16
fundraising, Book 4:16; Book 9:3, 15
job description, Book 1:2
meeting agenda, Book 8:7
meeting materials from, Book 9:14
micromanagement, Book 8:4, 5
mission understanding, Book 9:12–13
new board members, Book 9:13
nonprofit management career professional, Book 3:2–3
objectives, Book 1:2
organizational planning, Book 1:10
overstepping authority, Book 9:viii
personnel policies and procedures, Book 1:8
policy and planning, Book 9:1
public relations, Book 9:3
responsibilities, Book 8:5; Book 9:viii
retreat, Book 8:6–7
role of, Book 8:6–7
shared understanding of, Book 9:viii
sample job description, Book 9:19–20
search process, Book 1:2
selection, Book 1:2
sphere of influence, Book 8:vii
staff oversight, compensation, and evaluation, Book 9:3
structuring board materials, Book 8:6
structuring board meetings, Book 8:6
Civil law liability, Book 5:15
Code of ethics, Book 5:22
Cohesion, Book 3:5; Book 8:15
Collegiality, Book 3:6–7; Book 8:14
Commitment, Book 3:14
    values, Book 6:2
Committee, Book 3:19–20; Book 5:10. *See also* specific type of committee
    board chair, Book 9:2
    chief executive, Book 9:2
    liability, Book 5:10
    permanent standing committee, Book 3:7
    rotating committee assignments, Book 8:15
    types, Book 5:10
    work plan, Book 8:8
Committee meeting, Book 1:23
Communication, Book 1:15; Book 8:16

board chair, Book 9:3
board of directors, Book 3:20
chief executive, Book 9:3, 11
    to board of directors, Book 9:14
    to staff, Book 9:14
mission, Book 3:8–9; Book 6:3
program evaluation, Book 7:32

Community event, mission, Book 6:22–23

Community forum, Book 6:32–33

Community need
    fundraising, Book 4:1
    mission, Book 6:1, 19

Compensation
    chief executive, Book 2:5–6; Book 5:26
    excess benefit transaction, Book 5:26
    excessive, Book 5:26, 28
    staff, Book 2:5–6

Competition, Book 3:1–2
    for board members, Book 3:2
    by for-profit ventures, Book 3:2
    for resources, Book 3:1–2

Comprehensive strategic plan, chief executive, Book 8:6

Conditional promise to give, defined, Book 2:38

Conference call, board meeting, Book 5:9–10

Conflict, Book 1:23; Book 3:16, 30–31; Book 8:1

Conflict of interest, Book 1:8, 23
    appearance of, Book 2:7
    board member, Book 2:7
    confidential information, Book 2:7
    legality, Book 5:3–4, 21
    policy, Book 5:4, 21, 22
    staff, Book 2:7
    volunteer, Book 2:7

Consensus, Book 8:14

Consent agenda, Book 3:25; Book 8:10; Book 9:5

Consolidated financial statement, defined, Book 2:38

Constitution, unincorporated association, Book 5:7

Consultant
    fee increases, Book 2:22
    formal contract with, Book 2:28
    program evaluation, Book 7:29
    selection of, Book 2:27–28
    strategic planning, Book 7:17–18
    functions, Book 7:17
        selection, Book 7:17–18

Contingency plan, Book 8:16

Continuous board education, Book 5:20

Contract, Book 8:1

Contribution, defined, Book 2:38

Controller, role of, Book 2:16

Convention cancellation insurance, Book 2:25

Cooperation, Book 3:3

Corporation, Book 5:6–7
    articles of incorporation, Book 5:7
    bylaws, Book 5:7
    defined, Book 5:6
    liability, Book 5:6
    operational policies and procedures, Book 5:7
    state law, Book 5:7

Corruption, Book 3:2, 4–5

Cost-effectiveness guidelines, Book 4:25

Creativity, strategic planning, Book 7:2

Credit, Book 2:2

Criminal law liability, Book 5:15

Crisis, Book 8:1
    strategic planning, Book 7:4–5

Current planned gift, Book 4:5–6

Custodian fund, defined, Book 2:38

Customer feedback, mission statement, Book 6:3

D

Dashboard, defined, Book 7:22, 39

Dashboard report, Book 3:26, 38

Decision making, Book 5:20
    mission, Book 6:23

Deferred revenue, defined, Book 2:38
Depreciation, defined, Book 2:39
Designated, defined, Book 2:39
Development committee, Book 1:6
Development staff, Book 4:16–18
    functions, Book 4:16
Direct lobbying, Book 5:27
Direct mail, annual giving, Book 4:3
Director of development, Book 1:6
Director of finance, role of, Book 2:16
Directors' and officers' liability insurance, Book 2:26; Book 5:15
Disclaimed opinion, Book 2:21
Disclosure, tax-exempt organization, Book 5:26
Diversity, board of directors, Book 3:5
Donation, Book 5:26
Donor
    goals for giving, Book 4:13–14
    personal involvement, Book 4:9–10
Donor bill of rights, Book 4:36
Donor club, annual giving, Book 4:3
Donor cultivation, Book 4:12
    board member, Book 4:12
Donor development, Book 1:6
    building long-term relationship, Book 6:34
    issues-focused relationship, Book 6:34
    mission, Book 6:34
Donor-imposed condition, defined, Book 2:39
Donor-imposed restriction, defined, Book 2:39
Donor-investor, values, Book 6:34–35
Donor-recognition activity, Book 4:15
Donor-restricted endowment fund, defined, Book 2:39
Donor solicitation, Book 4:12–15
    board member
        fear of rejection, Book 4:13
            new board member, Book 4:12–13
            preparation, Book 4:13
            rehearsal, Book 4:13
    board-staff solicitation teams, Book 4:14–15
Donor stewardship, Book 6:32
Donor thanks, Book 4:15
Duty of care
    board member, Book 5:3
    negligence, Book 5:12
Duty of loyalty, board member, Book 5:3–4
Duty of obedience, board member, Book 5:4

E

Earned income, Book 3:4
Educational seminar, Book 5:20
Elevator speech exercise, Book 6:33
E-mail, Book 3:27
    mission, Book 6:32
Emergency plan, Book 8:16
Employment-related suit, Book 5:15
Endowment fund, defined, Book 2:39
English common law, Book 5:vii, 1
Enrollment marketing, Book 6:12
Errors and omissions insurance policy, Book 5:15
Estate planning, Book 4:5–6
Ethical integrity, Book 1:8
Evaluation, Book 1:vii. *See also* Program evaluation
    board meeting, Book 3:28–29, 40
    board member, Book 1:13
    board of directors, Book 1:13; Book 7:20; Book 8:10–12, 15; Book 9:9
    chief executive, Book 1:19–20; Book 9:6
        annual goals and objectives, Book 1:20
        processes, Book 1:20
        by third party, Book 1:20
    by constituents, Book 2:5–6
    continuous cycle, Book 7:37–38
    defined, Book 7:20
    frequency, Book 7:22–23
    fundraising, Book 4:15, 23–31
    cost of raising money, Book 4:27
        effective, Book 4:27, 28

efficient, Book 4:27, 28

goals, Book 4:23

performance criteria, Book 4:23–25

purposes and uses of gifts received, Book 4:27, 29

solicitation program results, Book 4:27, 30

sources of gifts, Book 4:27, 28

tracking growth, Book 4:23–25

hazards, Book 7:23–24

importance, Book 7:vii

key indicators of performance, Book 8:7

mission, Book 6:4

nonprofit organization, Book 3:6

 board role in, Book 3:6

 qualitative and subjective measures, Book 3:6

organizational effectiveness, Book 7:34–36

planning

 link between, Book 7:ix

 planning and evaluation cycle, Book 7:ix

 relationship, Book 7:20

questions asked, Book 7:23

rewards, Book 7:24

strategic planning, Book 7:17–18

timing, Book 7:22–23

value of, Book 7:37

Excess benefit transaction

 compensation, Book 5:26

 real property, Book 5:26

 safe harbor rules, Book 5:26

Exchange process

 mission statement, Book 6:12

 values, Book 6:12

Exchange transaction, defined, Book 2:39

Executive committee, Book 1:19

 disadvantages of, Book 3:20

Executive hour, Book 8:9

Executive search consultant, Book 1:2

Ex officio board member, Book 5:9

voting rights, Book 5:9

Expectations, communication of, Book 8:8–9

Expenses

 defined, Book 2:39

 expenditure propriety, Book 2:5–6

 natural classifications of, Book 2:4

revenue

 natural items of income and expenses in, Book 2:4

  programmatic perspective on, Book 2:3–4

  relationship between, Book 2:3–4

External audit, Book 2:12–13, 19–21

 auditor selection for, Book 2:12

 purposes of, Book 2:12

 review by external auditing firm, Book 2:12

F

Fair value, defined, Book 2:39

FASB (Financial Accounting Standards Board), defined, Book 2:39

Federal funding, requirements of, Book 2:7

Feedback, Book 8:10–12

 internal feedback mechanisms, Book 8:15

Fiduciary, defined, Book 2:39

Fiduciary responsibility, Book 5:vii, 1, 12

 concept of, Book 2:vi

 prudence, Book 5:vii

 reasonableness, Book 5:vii

Finance committee, Book 1:4

 audit, Book 1:4

 audit committee, distinguished, Book 3:21

 budget, Book 3:20–21

 financial statement, Book 2:19

 functions, Book 3:20–21

 role of, Book 2:14

Finances

 board chair, Book 9:1–2

 board of directors

  documents board should

receive, Book 2:18–22
    financial management responsibilities of, Book 2:14
    legal responsibility for, Book 2:14
chief executive, Book 9:2, 6, 15
    expert help with, Book 9:15
    responsibilities in, Book 2:15–16
decline of critical income sources, Book 2:22
increase of certain expenditures, Book 2:22
information, Book 2:18
signs of financial distress, Book 2:22–23
unplanned auditor turnover, Book 2:23
Financial crisis, Book 2:2
Financial planning, Book 2:1
    process of, Book 2:1
Financial statement
    certification, Book 5:22
    finance committee, Book 2:19
    frequency of, Book 2:19
    internally prepared, Book 2:19
501(c)(3) nonprofit organization, Book 5:5, 25
501(c)(4) social welfare organization, Book 5:6, 25
501(c)(6) professional society, Book 5:5–6, 25
501(c)(6) trade association, Book 5:5–6, 25
Fixed asset, defined, Book 2:40
For-profit business, profit as mission, Book 3:8
Foundation, major giving, Book 4:5
Friend raising, Book 4:14
Functional expenses, defined, Book 2:40
Fund, defined, Book 2:40
Fund accounting, Book 2:7
Fund balance, defined, Book 2:40
Fundraiser, Book 1:6
Fundraising, Book 1:6–7; Book 4:vii; Book 9:1
    associated functions, Book 4:27

board-appointed committees, Book 4:17
board chair, Book 9:3, 7–8
board member, Book 1:22
fundraising participation work sheet, Book 4:33
    personal giving, Book 4:10–11
    responsibilities, Book 4:34
board of directors
    oversight, Book 4:1–2
    responsibilities, Book 4:34
chief executive, Book 4:16; Book 9:3, 15
community needs, Book 4:1
concepts, Book 4:3–6
donor aspirations, Book 4:8
donor cultivation, Book 4:12
evaluation, Book 4:15, 23–31
    cost of raising money, Book 4:27
    effective, Book 4:27, 28
    efficient, Book 4:27, 28
    goals, Book 4:23
    performance criteria, Book 4:23–25
    purposes and uses of gifts received, Book 4:27, 29
    solicitation program results, Book 4:27, 30
    sources of gifts, Book 4:27, 28
    tracking growth, Book 4:23–25
integrated fundraising, defined, Book 4:9
investing time and money, Book 4:8–9
job description, Book 4:34
keys to effective, Book 4:19
mission, Book 4:1; Book 6:34–35
organizational structure, Book 4:16
paradigm shift, Book 6:34
programs and services, Book 4:1
pyramid of giving, Book 4:9–10
recruitment, Book 4:19–21
solicitation, Book 4:12–15
staff-led, staff-directed, staff-conducted, Book 4:17
stages, Book 4:12–18

strategic planning, Book 4:1
values, Book 4:1
vision, Book 4:1
Fundraising action plan, Book 4:1
Fundraising case statement, Book 1:6
Fundraising committee, Book 1:6
Fundraising consultant, Book 4:18
Fundraising expense, defined, Book 2:40
Fundraising regulation, Book 5:27
Fundraising workshop, Book 4:8
Future estate gift, Book 4:5–6

G

GAAP (generally accepted accounting principles), defined, Book 2:40
GAAS (generally accepted auditing standards), defined, Book 2:40
General liability policy, Book 5:15
Get-out-to-vote drive, Book 5:28
Gift acceptance, Book 8:1
Gift annuity, defined, Book 2:38
Gift-in-kind, defined, Book 2:40
Governance, Book 9:vii
    ineffective, reasons for, Book 3:30–33
    issues related to, Book 8:1
    lack of immediate rewards, Book 8:4
    management, distinction between, Book 8:vii
    mission-based, Book 3:8–9
Governance committee, Book 3:12–14
    board member prospect identification, Book 3:15
    board member recruitment, Book 1:13
    board orientation, Book 9:13
    functions, Book 1:13–14; Book 3:13
    fundraiser recruitment, Book 4:20–21
    importance, Book 1:13; Book 3:12–13
    mandate, Book 3:13
    self-assessment, Book 1:13, 14
Government report, Book 1:9
Grant
    defined, Book 2:40

    meeting funder's requirements, Book 2:6–7
Grass-roots lobbying, Book 5:27

H

Hearing Society, mission statement, Book 6:9

I

Immunity, Book 5:14
    state law, Book 5:14
Impact, defined, Book 7:21, 39
Inclusiveness, Book 8:15
Income, natural classifications of, Book 2:4
Incorporation, liability, Book 5:13
Indemnification, Book 5:13–14
    bylaws, Book 5:14
    insurance, Book 5:14
Independent audit, Book 5:19
Independent audit committee, Book 5:22
Independent contractor, Book 2:28
Indicator, defined, Book 7:21, 39
Informal advocacy
    mission, Book 6:33
    mission statement, Book 6:33
Information
    board chair, Book 9:7
    on finances, Book 2:18
Information collection, program evaluation, Book 7:30
Innovation, Book 9:11
Input, defined, Book 7:21, 39
In-service education, Book 1:21
Inspiration, Book 6:38
Insurance, Book 2:6, 25–26
    auditor, Book 2:6
    indemnification, Book 5:14
    liability, Book 5:15
    selection of, Book 2:25–26
    types, Book 2:25–26
Internal controls, Book 2:10–11
    auditor, Book 2:10–11
    in ensuring compliance, Book 2:7
    segregation of duties, Book 2:10

Investment, Book 2:26–27
    cash, Book 2:26
    decision on selection of, Book 2:27
    policies, Book 2:11–12
Investment committee, function of, Book 2:15
IRS Form 990, Book 2:5, 21; Book 5:25, 26
    defined, Book 2:40
Issue Definition and Policy Recommendation system, Book 3:26–27

J

Job description
    board member, Book 1:21; Book 4:34
    board of directors, Book 1:21
    fundraising, Book 4:34
Joint costs of multipurpose activities, defined, Book 2:40

L

Lawyer
    board member, Book 5:23
    role and responsibilities, Book 5:23–24
Leadership, Book 3:14; Book 6. *See also* Board chair
    board of directors, Book 8:4, 8, 15
    effective, Book 9:viii
    gray areas of, Book 9:1
    mission, Book 6:40–41
    mission drift, Book 6:21
    style of, Book 9:11
    succession, Book 6:40
Lease, Book 8:1
Legal integrity, Book 1:8
Letterhead board member, Book 9:9
Letter of Reportable Conditions, Book 2:21
Liability, Book 2:2
    board member, Book 5:1
    board vs. individual board member, Book 5:2
    collective and individual vigilance, Book 5:19–21
    corporation, Book 5:6, 13
    defined, Book 2:41
    employee's action, Book 5:12
    insurance, Book 5:15
    proactive governance, Book 5:13
    protective strategies, Book 5:13–15
    reasons for suits, Book 5:12
    trust (organizational form), Book 5:8
    unincorporated association, Book 5:7
Loan policy, Book 5:22
Lobbying, Book 1:9; Book 5:27
    safe harbor rule, Book 5:27
Long-range plan
    characterized, Book 7:8
    defined, Book 7:39
Loyalty, Book 3:14; Book 5:3–4

M

Mail ballot, Book 5:10
Major giving, Book 4:4–5
    capital campaign, Book 4:5
    corporations, Book 4:4
    foundation, Book 4:5
    individual donor, Book 4:6
    special-project campaign, Book 4:5
Management
    governance, distinction between, Book 8:vii
    issues related to, Book 8:1
    satisfaction from, Book 8:1
Management and general expense, defined, Book 2:41
Management Letter, Book 2:21
Mandate analysis, strategic planning, Book 7:12
Marketing, mission statement, Book 6:11–13
Market survey, mission, Book 6:19
Members' audit, Book 2:12–13
Membership development expense, defined, Book 2:41
Membership program, annual giving, Book 4:3
Micromanagement, Book 2:23
    all-volunteer organization, Book 8:5

board of directors, Book 8:4
chair, Book 8:5
characterized, Book 8:4
chief executive, Book 8:4, 5
indications of, Book 8:4–5
reasons for, Book 8:4

Minutes, board meeting, Book 3:26, 28; Book 5:20
    wording of motions, Book 3:28

Miscellaneous expense account, increasing, Book 2:22

Mismanagement, Book 3:2, 4–5

Mission, Book 5:4; Book 9:1, 6–7
    advocacy, Book 6:31–33
    articulating, Book 6:3
    board chair, Book 6:40–41
    board meeting review, Book 6:20
    board member, Book 5:17–18
    board of directors, Book 6:2–3
    board member agreement, Book 6:19–20
        role, Book 6:18–23
    board recruitment, Book 6:36–37, 42
    board-staff partnership, Book 6:18
    chief executive, Book 9:12–13
    communication, Book 3:8–9; Book 6:3
    community event, Book 6:22–23
    community need, Book 6:1, 19
    conceptual basis, Book 6:1
    decision making, Book 6:23
    defined, Book 3:8; Book 6:6
    developing consensus on, Book 9:viii
    development process, Book 6:3
    donor development, Book 6:34
    e-mail, Book 6:32
    evaluation, Book 6:4
    fundraising, Book 4:1; Book 6:34–35
    identification, Book 1:1; Book 6:18–23
    importance, Book 3:8; Book 6:vii
    informal advocacy, Book 6:33
    as inspiration, Book 6:28
    leadership, Book 6:40–41
    market survey, Book 6:19
    as measure of relevance, Book 6:4
    motivation, Book 6:13, 20–21
    programs and services, Book 1:17
    reinvented, Book 6:4
    relating vision to mission, Book 6:15
    retreat, Book 6:22; Book 9:viii
    review, Book 1:1
    role, Book 6:1–4
    shared understanding of, Book 9:viii,12–13
    staff development process, Book 6:18
    stakeholder, Book 1:1
    stewardship, Book 6:35
    strategic planning, Book 6:28–29
    uniqueness, Book 6:vii
    US Canoe and Kayak Team, Book 3:9, 10–11
    validity over time, Book 6:42–43
    values, Book 6:1, 16
    Web site, Book 6:31

Mission drift, Book 6:19–20, 21
    board turnover, Book 6:39
    leadership, Book 6:21
    sources, Book 6:21
    symptoms, Book 6:21

Mission driven, defined, Book 6:1–2

Mission focused, defined, Book 6:1–2

Mission statement, Book 1:1; Book 3:9; Book 5:17; Book 6:3, 6; Book 8:8
    board of directors, Book 8:8
    characteristics of excellence, Book 6:6
    corporate-sounding, Book 6:10
    customer feedback, Book 6:3
    defined, Book 6:6; Book 7:40
    development, Book 6:9–11, 19–23
    emotionally powerful, Book 6:6–10
    advantages, Book 6:10–11
    exchange process, Book 6:12
    Hearing Society, Book 6:9
    identifying mission, Book 6:8–10
    informal advocacy, Book 6:33
    internal uses, Book 6:13
    as marketing tool, Book 6:11–13
    motivation, Book 6:13
    public speaking, Book 6:32–33

purpose, Book 6:7, 8
purpose-specific, Book 6:8
review, Book 1:1
revision, Book 6:25
staff role, Book 6:18
Science Museum of Minnesota, Book 6:9
strategic planning, Book 7:15
tone, Book 6:10–11
uses, Book 1:1; Book 6:7
values, Book 6:6, 7
Vector Health Program, Book 6:7, 10–11
why statement and what statement, Book 6:6–7, 8
writing process, Book 6:10–11, 25–27
    creating draft committee, Book 6:25
    discussing values, Book 6:25
    feedback, Book 6:26
    final board approval, Book 6:26
    identifying values, Book 6:25
    polishing process, Book 6:26
    preliminary board approval, Book 6:26
    reviewing first draft, Book 6:26
Yale University School of Medicine, Book 6:7–8
Motivation, Book 3:33
    board meeting, Book 6:20–21
    mission, Book 6:13, 20–21
    mission statement, Book 6:13
    orientation, Book 6:38–39
    staff, Book 6:13
    strategic planning, Book 7:3

N

Natural expenses, defined, Book 2:41
Needs-based allocation, Book 3:5–6
Net assets, defined, Book 2:41
New philanthropy, Book 6:2
Newsletter, Book 6:32
Nominating committee, Book 3:5. *See also* Governance committee
board orientation, Book 9:13
Nonprofit organization, Book 5:5–8, 27. *See also* All-volunteer organization; Tax-exempt organization
    accounting in, Book 2:4, 18
    career professionals in, Book 3:2–3
    control vs. ownership, Book 5:9
    core values of, Book 8:14
    critical income sources declining, Book 2:22
    emerging trends, Book 3:1–7
    entrepreneurial opportunities and risks, Book 3:3–4
    evaluation, Book 3:6
    board role in, Book 3:6
        qualitative and subjective measures, Book 3:6
    expectations for demonstrable achievements, Book 3:1
    growth drivers, Book 3:1
    hallmark characteristics, Book 8:14
    hard drivers of success, Book 6:16
    increasing expenditures, Book 2:22
    insuring against risks, Book 2:6
    issues-based investment and involvement, Book 6:2
    more professional, Book 3:2–3
    most important issues, Book 8:2
    number, Book 3:1
    organizational form, Book 5:6–8
    profitable ventures, Book 3:4
    in public eye, Book 2:5
    related entities, Book 5:19
    results driven, Book 3:5–6
    signs of financial distress, Book 2:22–23
    small or young, without staff, Book 8:3
    soft drivers of success, Book 6:16
    surplus in, Book 2:4
    systems protecting, Book 2:10–13
    tax and information filing calendar
    for federal filings, Book 2:32
    for state filings, Book 2:33

welfare of, Book 8:8

Nonprofit organization management, as professional career, Book 3:2–3

Nonreciprocal transfer, defined, Book 2:41

Not-for-profit organization, defined, Book 2:41

O

Objectives, defined, Book 7:40

Officer, nomination, Book 3:13, 15

Official spokesperson, Book 9:3

OMB A-133 audit, Book 2:21–22

OMB Circular A-133, defined, Book 2:41

Online fundraising, Book 5:27

Open meeting laws, Book 5:28–29

Operating budget, Book 5:5

Operational/action/tactical plan, defined, Book 7:40

Operational details, Book 8:viii

Operational plan, characterized, Book 7:7

Operational policies and procedures, corporation, Book 5:7

Operational reserves, defined, Book 2:41

Organizational agenda, Book 8:7

Organizational culture, Book 8:14
    strategic planning, Book 7:3

Organizational effectiveness
    board of directors, Book 7:34
    evaluation, Book 7:22, 34–36, 40
    goals and objectives, Book 7:35
    outcomes measurement, Book 7:34–35
    program evaluation, Book 7:34–35
    strategic planning, Book 7:35
    SWOT analysis, Book 7:35

Organizational planning, Book 1:10–11
    board of directors, Book 1:10
    chief executive, Book 1:10
    elements, Book 1:11
    principles, Book 1:10
    staff, Book 1:10

Organization manager, Book 5:8

Orientation, Book 5:20; Book 6:37–39; Book 8:14
    board chair, Book 9:2
    board member, Book 8:8–9
    to board, Book 1:13
    to organization, Book 1:13
    board of directors, Book 3:13–14, 15
    orientation meeting, Book 3:14
    written materials, Book 3:13–14
    chief executive, Book 9:2, 13
    components, Book 6:38
    governance committee, Book 9:13
    information, Book 6:38
    inspiration, Book 6:38
    motivation, Book 6:38–39
    nominating committee, Book 9:13
    outcomes, Book 6:39
    setting standards, Book 6:37
    values, Book 6:38

Outcome, Book 7:21, 34–35
    defined, Book 7:21, 40

Outcomes measurement
    defined, Book 7:22, 40
    organizational effectiveness, Book 7:34–35
    program evaluation, Book 7:26, 27, 29–30, 31

Output, defined, Book 7:21, 40

Outside advisor
    formal contract with, Book 2:28
    selection of, Book 2:27–28

P

Partnership, Book 3:3

Perceptual analysis, strategic planning, Book 7:12

Performance evaluation. *See also* Evaluation
    board member, Book 3:16

Performance measurement
    defined, Book 7:22, 40
    program evaluation, Book 7:30, 31

Permanently restricted net assets, defined, Book 2:42

Permanent restriction, defined, Book 2:42

Personal agenda, board member, Book 3:16, 31
Personal liability, Book 5:1, 12
Personnel committee, Book 2:14–15
Personnel costs, Book 2:4
Personnel policies and procedures, Book 1:8, 9
    chief executive, Book 1:8
Planned giving, Book 4:5–6
Planning
    board chair, Book 9:1
    board of directors, Book 7:viii
    chief executive, Book 9:1
    continuous cycle, Book 7:37–38
    evaluation
    link between, Book 7:ix
    planning and evaluation cycle, Book 7:ix
    relationship, Book 7:20
    importance, Book 7:vii
Planning committee, strategic planning, Book 7:10
    committee deliberation, Book 7:13–14
    SWOT analysis, Book 7:13
Plant fund, defined, Book 2:42
Pledge, defined, Book 2:42
Policy, Book 8:vii
    board chair, Book 9:1
    chief executive, Book 9:1
    difficulties of setting, Book 8:1–2
    objectives, Book 8:18
    policy compendium, Book 3:27
Political campaign activities, Book 5:28
Political education campaign, Book 5:28
Prepaid expense, defined, Book 2:42
President, Book 6. *See* Board chair
Press release, Book 1:15
Printed material, Book 6:32
Private benefit, Book 5:28
Private foundation, Book 5:6, 25
Private inurement, Book 2:22–23; Book 5:28
    board member, Book 2:6, 7
    defined, Book 2:42

disqualified persons, Book 5:28
Proactive governance, Book 5:13
Professional society, Book 5:5–6, 25
Program evaluation. *See also* Evaluation
    board of directors, Book 7:28
    communication, Book 7:32
    constituents in, Book 7:29
    consultant, Book 7:29
    defined, Book 7:22, 40
    frequency, Book 7:26–28
    importance, Book 7:26
    information collection, Book 7:30
    organizational effectiveness, Book 7:34–35
    outcomes measurement, Book 7:26, 27, 29–30, 31
    performance measurement, Book 7:30, 31
    results, Book 7:32
    staff, Book 7:28–29
    timing, Book 7:26–28
Program expense, defined, Book 2:42
Program/project plan, defined, Book 7:41
Programs and services
    board of directors, monitoring and oversight role, Book 1:17
    confused board and staff roles, Book 1:17
    fundraising, Book 4:1
    mission, Book 1:17
    quality, Book 1:17
Promise to give, defined, Book 2:42
Proposal, board meeting, Book 3:26
    Issue Definition and Policy Recommendation system, Book 3:26–27
Propriety, appearance of, Book 2:5
Prospect identification, Book 4:12, 14
Prospect qualification, Book 4:12
Proxy, Book 5:10
Public advocacy group, Book 5:6, 25
Public charity, Book 5:6, 25
Public foundation. *See* Public charity
Public relations

board chair, Book 9:3
chief executive, Book 9:3
public relations program, Book 1:15
Public speaking, Book 1:15
mission statement, Book 6:32–33
Pyramid of giving, Book 4:9–10

Q

Qualified opinion, Book 2:20–21
Quasi-endowment fund, defined, Book 2:42
Quorum, board meeting, Book 5:9

R

Real property, excess benefit transaction, Book 5:26
Reclassification, defined, Book 2:42
Regulatory environment, Book 5:vi
Regulatory requirements, Book 5:4
Related entities, Book 5:19
Reporting guidelines, Book 5:4; Book 8:4
Reserves, Book 2:2–3
appropriate level of, Book 2:3
defined, Book 2:2
restricted support, Book 2:3
Resources, Book 1:6–7
competition for, Book 3:1–2
sources, Book 1:7
stability, Book 1:7
Restricted endowment fund, defined, Book 2:39
Restricted funds, funder's requirements, Book 2:6–7
Restricted support
defined, Book 2:42
reserves, Book 2:3
Results-based evaluation, Book 3:5–6
Retreat, Book 3:5, 16; Book 8:15; Book 9:7
chief executive, Book 8:6–7
mission, Book 6:22
testimonial, Book 6:22
Revenue, Book 1:7
defined, Book 2:43
expenses
natural items of income and expenses in, Book 2:4
programmatic perspective on, Book 2:3–4
relationship between, Book 2:3–4
revenue-generating activities, Book 1:7
sources, Book 4:vii
Roll call vote, Book 3:28
Rules of order, board meeting, Book 3:27–28

S

Safe harbor rules, Book 5:19, 26, 27
Salary, increasing, Book 2:22
Sarbanes-Oxley Act of 2002, Book 5:vi
Science Museum of Minnesota, mission statement, Book 6:9
Self-assessment, Book 8:9, 10–12, 15; Book 9:2
board of directors, Book 3:31–32
benefits, Book 3:32
commitment, Book 3:31
mini self-assessment survey, Book 3:32, 39–41
outside facilitation, Book 3:32
Shared governance, Book 8:14
Signature authorization, Book 8:1
Small organization, managing without staff, Book 8:3
Social entrepreneurship, Book 3:3–4
Social indicator, defined, Book 7:21, 41
Social welfare group, Book 5:6, 25
Special event, annual giving, Book 4:4
Special-project campaign, major giving, Book 4:5
Spending rate, defined, Book 2:43
Split-interest gift, defined, Book 2:43
Spokesperson
board chair, Book 3:14
inappropriate and unilateral initiatives, Book 1:15
selection, Book 1:15
Sponsorship, Book 3:3
Staff, Book 4. *See also* Development staff
authority, Book 5:9

benefits, Book 2:5–6
board chair, Book 9:3
board meeting, participation in, Book 8:7
board member
    micromanagement by, Book 9:vii
    relationship, Book 1:23; Book 5:21
board of directors
    creating strong partnerships, Book 9:12
    relationship, Book 1:viii; Book 8:3, 16
    role differentiation, Book 8:4–5
board-staff solicitation teams, Book 4:14–15
chief executive, Book 9:3
compensation, Book 2:5–6
conflict of interest, Book 2:7
improperly handled legal matter, Book 5:23
mission development process, Book 6:18
more professional, Book 3:2–3
motivation, Book 6:13
nonprofit management career professionals, Book 3:2–3
organizational planning, Book 1:10
overstepping authority, Book 9:viii
program evaluation, Book 7:28–29
responsibilities, Book 8:7
role clarification, Book 8:4
small nonprofit organization, Book 8:3
strategic planning, Book 7:14
turnover rates, Book 9:13
Stakeholder, Book 8:16
    defined, Book 7:41
    mission, Book 1:1
    strategic planning, Book 7:12
Standing committee, Book 3:19–20
Stanford University, vision, Book 6:16
State law
    corporation, Book 5:7
    immunity, Book 5:14
    tax-exempt organization, Book 5:29

    trust (organizational form), Book 5:8
    unincorporated association, Book 5:7
Stewardship, Book 4:15
    mission, Book 6:35
Stipulation, defined, Book 2:43
Strategic goal, defined, Book 7:41
Strategic planning, Book 8:17
    approaches, Book 7:8–9
    board's role, Book 7:3
    bylaws, Book 7:12
    change, Book 7:1–2
    competitive analysis, Book 7:12–13
    consultant, Book 7:17–18
    functions, Book 7:17
    selection, Book 7:17–18
    creativity, Book 7:2
    crisis, Book 7:4–5
    critical issues approach, Book 7:9, 10–14
    defined, Book 7:9, 41
    elements, Book 1:11
    environmental scan of external world, Book 7:12
    establishing priorities, Book 8:17
    evaluation, Book 7:17–18
    fundraising, Book 4:1
    getting started, Book 7:10
    importance, Book 7:3–4
    information gathering and analysis, Book 7:11–13
    management goals approach, Book 7:8
    mandate analysis, Book 7:12
    mission, Book 6:28–29
    mission statement, Book 7:15
    motivation, Book 7:3
    nature of, Book 7:2–3
    negative aspects, Book 7:1
    objectives, Book 7:16
    organizational culture, Book 7:3
    organizational effectiveness, Book 7:35
    overview, Book 7:1–2
    perceptual analysis, Book 7:12
    performance measures, Book 7:16–17
    planning committee, Book 7:10

committee deliberation, Book 7:13–14
SWOT analysis, Book 7:13
planning to plan, Book 7:10–11
readiness of board and staff, Book 7:4
scenario approach, Book 7:8–9
staff, Book 7:14
stakeholder, Book 7:12
strategic goals, Book 7:15–16
strategic plan contents, Book 7:14–17
strategies, Book 7:16
time frame, Book 7:2
unsuitable, Book 7:4–5
values, Book 7:15
vision, Book 6:28–29; Book 7:1
vision statement, Book 7:15
Strategy, Book 8:vii
difficulties of setting, Book 8:1–2
Subsidiary, Book 5:28
Sunshine laws, Book 5:28–29
Supporting expense, defined, Book 2:43
SWOT analysis, Book 7:13
defined, Book 7:41
organizational effectiveness, Book 7:35

T

Tactical plan, characterized, Book 7:7
Task force, Book 3:7
functions, Book 3:19–20
work plan, Book 8:8
Taxes, tax and information filing calendar, Book 2:32
for federal filings, Book 2:32
for state filings, Book 2:33
Tax-exempt, defined, Book 2:43
Tax-exempt organization, Book 5:29. *See also* Nonprofit organization
defined, Book 5:5, 25
disclosure, Book 5:26
intermediate sanctions, Book 5:27
IRS regulations, Book 5:18
state law, Book 5:29
subsidiary, Book 5:28

unrelated business activities, Book 5:29
variations, Book 5:5
Teamwork, Book 3:5
Telephone contact, annual giving, Book 4:4
Temporarily restricted net assets, defined, Book 2:43
Temporary restriction, defined, Book 2:43
Term endowment, defined, Book 2:43
Term limits, Book 3:16
Testamentary trust, Book 5:8
Testimonial
board meeting, Book 6:20
retreat, Book 6:22
Total return approach, defined, Book 2:43
Trade association, Book 5:5–6, 25
Transaction, Book 6:34–35
Transformation, Book 6:34–35
Treasurer, Book 1:4
bonding, Book 2:15
role of, Book 2:15
Trust, Book 9:12
communication, Book 9:ix
importance of, Book 9:ix
Trustee. *See* Board of directors
Trust (organizational form), Book 5:8
liability, Book 5:8
state law, Book 5:8

U

Uncertain, defined, Book 2:43
Unconditional promise to give, defined, Book 2:43
Unincorporated association, Book 5:7
bylaws, Book 5:7
constitution, Book 5:7
liability, Book 5:7
state law, Book 5:7
Unrelated business activities, Book 5:29
Unrelated business income, Book 1:7
defined, Book 2:44
Unrestricted net assets, defined, Book 2:44
Unrestricted support, defined, Book 2:44

US Canoe and Kayak Team
    mission, Book 3:9, 10–11
    values, Book 3:9

V

Values
    board recruitment, Book 6:36–37, 42
    characterized, Book 6:2
    commitment, Book 6:2
    creating, Book 3:9
    donor-investor, Book 6:34–35
    exchange process, Book 6:12
    fundraising, Book 4:1
    mission, Book 6:1, 16
    mission statement, Book 6:6, 7, 25
    orientation, Book 6:38
    purpose, Book 3:9
    range of, Book 6:2
    strategic planning, Book 7:15
    US Canoe and Kayak Team, Book 3:9
    vision, Book 6:16
Values based, defined, Book 6:1–2
Values-based marketing, by corporate sector, Book 6:11–12
Values statement, defined, Book 7:41
Vector Health Program, mission statement, Book 6:7, 10–11
Vision, Book 9:6–7
    for community, Book 6:16
    defined, Book 6:15–16
    developing consensus on, Book 9:viii
    fundraising, Book 4:1
    for organization, Book 6:15–16
    purpose, Book 3:9
    relating vision to mission, Book 6:15
    retreat, Book 9:viii
    shared understanding of, Book 9:viii
    Stanford University, Book 6:16
    strategic planning, Book 6:28–29; Book 7:1
    values, Book 6:16
Vision statement
    defined, Book 6:15; Book 7:41
    strategic planning, Book 7:15

Volunteer, Book 5:14
    conflict of interest, Book 2:7
Volunteer Protection Act of 1997, Book 5:14

W

Web-based giving, Book 4:4
Web site, mission, Book 6:31
Why mission statement, Book 6:6–10
Work plan
    board of directors, Book 8:8
    committee, Book 8:8
    task force, Book 8:8
Written materials, board meeting, Book 3:24, 25

Y

Yale University School of Medicine, mission statement, Book 6:7–8